# The Hidden Inequities in Labor-Based Contract Grading

# Current Arguments in Composition

Utah State University Press's Current Arguments in Composition is a series of short-form publications of provocative original material and selections from foundational titles by leading thinkers in the field. Perfect for the composition classroom as well as the professional collection, this series provides access to important introductory content as well as innovative new work intended to stimulate scholarly conversation. Volumes are available in paperback or ebook form.

*The Hidden Inequities in Labor-Based Contract Grading*
ELLEN C. CARILLO

*Nowhere Near the Line: Pain and Possibility in Teaching and Writing*
ELIZABETH BOQUET

*Post-Truth Rhetoric and Composition*
BRUCE MCCOMISKEY

*The Problem with Education Technology (Hint: It's Not the Technology)*
BEN FINK AND ROBIN BROWN

# The Hidden Inequities in Labor-Based Contract Grading

Ellen C. Carillo

Utah State University Press
*Logan*

© 2021 by University Press of Colorado

Published by Utah State University Press
An imprint of University Press of Colorado
245 Century Circle, Suite 202
Louisville, Colorado 80027

USU Press Current Arguments in Composition

 The University Press of Colorado is a proud member of
the Association of University Presses.

The University Press of Colorado is a cooperative publishing enterprise supported,
in part, by Adams State University, Colorado State University, Fort Lewis College,
Metropolitan State University of Denver, Regis University, University of Alaska
Fairbanks, University of Colorado, University of Denver, University of Northern
Colorado, University of Wyoming, Utah State University, and Western Colorado
University.

∞ This paper meets the requirements of the ANSI/NISO Z39.48–1992 (Permanence of Paper).

ISBN: 978-1-64642-266-1 (paperback)
ISBN: 978-1-64642-267-8 (ebook)
https://doi.org/10.7330/9781646422678

Library of Congress Cataloging-in-Publication Data

Names: Carillo, Ellen C., author.
Title: The hidden inequities in labor-based contract grading / Ellen C. Carillo.
Other titles: Current arguments in composition.
Description: Logan : Utah State University Press, [2021] | Series: Current arguments
    in composition | Includes bibliographical references and index.
Identifiers: LCCN 2021035839 (print) | LCCN 2021035840 (ebook) | ISBN
    9781646422661 (paperback) | ISBN 9781646422678 (ebook)
Subjects: LCSH: English language—Rhetoric—Ability testing—United States. |
    College students—Rating of. | Learning—Evaluation. | Academic writing—Evaluation. | Grading and marking (Students)—United States.
Classification: LCC LB2368 .C37 2021 (print) | LCC LB2368 (ebook) | DDC
    371.27/20973—dc23
LC record available at https://lccn.loc.gov/2021035839
LC ebook record available at https://lccn.loc.gov/2021035840

# Contents

# Acknowledgments

I am especially grateful to the two anonymous reviewers who provided insightful and detailed feedback on this project. I am also indebted to Michael Spooner, who developed the Current Arguments in Composition series years ago, and Rachael Levay, who recognized that this manuscript was a good fit for it. I would also like to thank Rachael for her thoughtful advice and guidance in the early stages of this project and, more generally, for her steadfast support of my scholarship. As always, I am grateful to the wonderful team at Utah State University Press for preparing this manuscript for publication.

# The Hidden Inequities in Labor-Based Contract Grading

# Introduction

Since the start of the COVID-19 pandemic in March 2020, there has been more widespread attention to grading practices than ever before. Schools nationwide adjusted their approaches to grading, including their grading scales and procedures. Many postsecondary institutions, in particular, gave students a great deal of choice regarding how they would be assessed. Students could choose, for example, whether they wanted to receive a letter grade or take their courses on a pass/fail basis. At some institutions, students could view their letter grades first and then make this choice, giving students maximum flexibility. Students were also given more time to withdraw from courses with limited or no consequences, and some institutions even invented new grading protocols wherein grades were accompanied by a specific marker that reminds anyone reviewing that academic transcript that those courses were taken during the pandemic.

I am not suggesting that this heightened attention to grading was an outgrowth of deep and prolonged engagement with the research and scholarship on grading practices. It was, instead, a very pragmatic response to a pandemic that posed a range of challenges for students and disproportionately so for students of color. Still, this was a moment wherein grading—on perhaps the largest scale we can imagine—ceased to be taken for granted. The status quo was disrupted. Of course, those in education, writing studies, educational psychology, and other fields have never taken grading for granted. Studying assessment practices has always been an important part of the research and scholarship in these fields. By the time this manuscript is published, grading practices will likely have reverted to their seemingly unproblematic pre-pandemic status. I would hope, though, that the complexities associated with grading (both on this large scale and at the more local level in our classrooms) exposed by the pandemic might lead to some change, particularly when considered alongside the systemic racism embedded across institutions in the United States that the pandemic also underscored and exacerbated.

With racial disparities at the forefront of Americans' minds, and further magnified by the murder of George Floyd in the early months of the pandemic, many instructors, including those at the postsecondary level, found themselves reflecting on their role in perpetuating these injustices. Although antiracist pedagogy is not without its detractors, many postsecondary instructors across the country began committing themselves to becoming antiracist educators who deliberately sought to dismantle the educational structures that contributed to racism. Part of this work involved revisiting and revising their assessment practices.

One form of assessment that emerged well before 2020 but gained much more traction in light of the spotlight on racial disparities in American culture is labor-based contract grading. This form of assessment has been popularized most consistently and recently by scholar-teacher Asao Inoue, who has been an invaluable leader in writing studies as the field contends with grading practices that perpetuate a single, dominant standard. Inoue and others, including Wonderful Faison, Carmen Kynard, Mya Poe, and Vershawn Ashanti Young have pointed out how these and related pedagogical practices can impede learning and are disproportionately harmful to students of color and raciolinguistically diverse students. This population of students is especially important to me as I teach and direct a writing program at a campus where 48 percent of students identify as students of color and 51 percent report being first-generation college students. While the campus does not have statistics on the linguistic diversity of students, in my own experience teaching at the institution for close to fifteen years, I would say that at least 50 percent of students in each class that I teach speak a language other than English. Over the years, those languages have included Spanish, Russian, Albanian, and Farsi with an increasing number of students who speak Chinese. As such, these discussions surrounding how assessment practices affect racially and linguistically diverse students are especially relevant to my own teaching. In fact, my commitment to this population of students compelled me to enter this discussion. In particular, I am invested in contributing to the already rich conversation about labor-based contract grading, a form of assessment that has now been adopted by instructors across the country.

I was also moved to enter this conversation because of Inoue's openness in Chapter 6 of *Labor-Based Contract Grading: Building Equity and Inclusion in the Compassionate Writing Classroom* to critiques and questions about labor-based contract grading. Inoue (2019, 18) describes the chapter as a "kind of FAQ" that "contains fourteen questions concerning the use of labor-based grading contracts . . . gathered from various teachers and others from across the US and on the WPA-L [Writing Program Administrators' Listserv]." In that chapter, Inoue (2019) welcomes opportunities to improve his assessment practices so that they are informed by scholarship in disability studies. Inoue (2019, 228) notes that "a good assessment ecology, one that is socially just in every way, should be self-consciously designed to meet the principles of universal design." Moreover, he admits that "in terms of the scholarship and impressive work being done around UDL [Universal Design for Learning] and disability studies, I am still learning and perhaps most excited about ways it may help improve labor-based grading contracts. I feel I have a lot to learn and perhaps to alter in my own practices" (229). This essay takes Inoue's call seriously, picking up this thread in order to explore—through a disability studies lens—some of the shortcomings in current iterations of labor-based grading contracts, which Inoue seems to anticipate above.

The goal of this extended essay is to further enrich the conversation surrounding labor-based contract grading by expanding its scope. To do so, I explore some of the assumptions inherent in labor-based contract grading and highlight the groups of students, including students with disabilities and students that are twice or more marginalized, that remain disadvantaged by this increasingly popular assessment practice. Specifically, I draw on the field of disability studies, recognizing that "disability enables insight—critical, experiential, cognitive, sensory, and pedagogical insight" (Brueggeman 2001, 795). I will suggest some avenues those of us in writing studies might pursue, such as developing engagement-based grading contracts, in order to address the shortcomings I outline surrounding labor-based contract grading. In keeping with the approach of its predecessors in the series, though, this essay will primarily define, describe, and consider the implications of these problems.

Arguing for assessment practices that address the growing number of students with physical disabilities, as well as students with neurodivergent conditions, including anxiety and depression, this essay contributes to efforts toward creating more equitable assessment practices in our classrooms. Ultimately, there is important research to be done on grading contracts, and it can't come soon enough. Indebted to those who have looked at this issue from the perspective of racial formations, this essay explores the nonracially motivated standards and biases that are exposed when we take a closer look at labor-based grading contracts.

## A BRIEF HISTORY OF CONTRACT GRADING

According to "A Legacy of Grading Contracts for Composition," Michelle Cowan's (2020) incredibly comprehensive, century-long history and examination of grading contracts, this form of assessment been used in classrooms since the 1920s. However, it was in the 1960s and 1970s that we begin to see an increase in the number of articles on grading contracts—or what were then often called learning contracts. Most articles on the subject were published in the field of education (both secondary and postsecondary), but in the developing field of composition, Peter Elbow emerged as a pioneer, publishing "A Method for Teaching English" in 1968. Elbow's article outlines an approach to including students in both the development of the curriculum and in assessment practices. The kinds of contracts described in scholarship from this period varied widely with some scholar-teachers reporting their development of full-class contracts and many others focused on individualized contracts meant to promote self-directed learning. The ways in which students contributed to these contracts also varied: in some cases, students were involved in the creation and negotiation of the contracts while in other cases instructors developed the contracts independently of input from students. While instructors reported different reasons for adopting learning contracts, Cowan points out that many instructors were compelled by their investment in seeking fairer and more transparent forms of assessment. Some teacher-scholars, like Elbow, were looking for ways to circumvent traditional grading altogether.

Although contracts continued to vary widely, as they do today, with the rise of the process movement in the field of composition over the next two decades, contracts often reflected an emphasis on practicality, and, in writing courses specifically, focused on students' goals and processes rather than their products (Cowan). It's not until the 1990s that instructors began to consistently and deliberately situate these contracts as "instruments of emancipation" (Cowan) and a means to more socially just and anti-oppressive teaching and grading practices. Around the turn of the twenty-first century, this approach to assessment began coalescing into a form we would recognize today with three major categories of grading contracts: contracts based on the quality of students' work; contracts based on the labor students expended to complete the work; and hybrid contracts that value both labor and quality.

In this essay, I am interested in considering labor-based grading contracts specifically, and the role they are intended to play in creating more socially just forms of assessment. While writing within the contemporary moment does not afford me the perspective Cowan was afforded in her historical study of this assessment practice, I have become concerned with how labor-based grading contracts, which are intended to promote equality and social justice, unintentionally privilege some students over others. This project seeks to draw others' attention to this issue and encourages instructors, both within and beyond writing studies—and even beyond the humanities—to create assessments that recognize students' intersectional identities and are inclusive of students with various disabilities.

# 1

## Assumptions in Labor-Based Contract Grading

As I suggest in the introduction, the issues I outline with labor-based contract grading are not necessarily within the scope of the important and impressive work that has already been done in this area to help move instructors toward antiracist pedagogies and assessment practices. My aim, then, is to open new pathways for "trying not to be unfair" (Inoue 2019, 11) in our classrooms by drawing attention to the need to expand the scope of the discussion beyond race and language while remaining mindful of how the current focus on race and language can guide us in important ways. While we don't want to forget the importance of our contemporary context and the racial injustices that we must address, expanding the scope of the discussion allows us to explore populations of students that must be taken into consideration when creating assessments so that we "can ensure equitable and inclusive practices in inherently unfair systems that are by their nature inequitable and exclusive" (Inoue 2019, 11). Looking at some of the assumptions inherent in labor-based contract grading practices lays the foundation for this work.

While grading contracts are often idiosyncratic (Cowan 2020) to individual instructors, Inoue's labor-based grading contract has captured the field's attention and incited writing instructors and writing programs across the country to adopt this approach to assessment (e.g., Langston University, University of Connecticut, Texas A&M University-San Antonio, Western Washington University, Humboldt University). Certainly not all labor-based grading contracts will look like the version popularized by Inoue and explored most comprehensively in his book titled *Labor-Based Contract Grading: Building Equity and Inclusion in the Compassionate Writing Classroom*, but this version, which has become the exemplar for many in writing studies, will play a major role in my discussion of this assessment practice.

Inoue (2019, 46) explains that labor-based grading contracts are necessary because more common grading schemes that consider the quality of students' work as opposed to their labor (or in addition to labor) are relying on a single standard of "quality that is determined by a racialized group in power, a White, middle-class group." He explains further: "Grading by a single standard is how most, if not all, schools and writing classrooms exercise the historical right to exclude in order to protect literacy as White property. . . . Put more directly, in all schools, grades are the means of discrimination, the methods of exclusion, not inclusion, no matter what else we may think they do for our students" (2019, 11). Inoue turns, instead, to labor, which he defines as "the work done in and for a course, that is, the bodily work of reading, writing, and other activities associated with what it takes to engage in a writing course" (2019, 78). Labor seems attractive to Inoue because it is quantifiable while quality is not. "The use of labor-based grading contracts, I believe," further explains Inoue (2019, 8), "changes the rules of the grading game in such a way that White language supremacy can not only be seen for what it is, but effectively countered. This makes for a fairer, more equitable, and inclusive language classroom."

In Inoue's classes, and in any classes that adopt labor-based grading contracts in their purest sense, labor is the sole assessment measure. In these classes, students are often asked to record all of their labor by tracking the number of minutes spent on each task. In Inoue's classes, estimates of the amount of labor necessary for each task within each assignment are shared with students as part of the assignment: "All labor is quantified in words read or written, and in estimated time a student is expected to spend on the activity, which is also broken up into steps with duration per step also listed" (Inoue 2019, 130).

When labor is quantified in this way, though, labor-based contract grading inaccurately assumes that labor is a neutral measure—or at least that it is less inequitable a measure than quality. The suggestion is that because labor is more easily quantifiable than quality, labor offers a more equitable form of assessment. Underscoring this point, Inoue (2019, 131) notes: "One hour of labor is worth one hour of labor, regardless of the kind of labor you are engaged in during that hour."

However, while labor-based grading contracts may help mitigate the structural injustices perpetuated on some students by the grading system, unfortunately, these contracts perpetuate injustices for other students. These contracts enforce a White, middle-class, and, most important for my purposes, normative, ableist, and neurotypical conception of labor. Consider, for example, who is at the center of this grading philosophy, the contracts themselves, or even at the center of Inoue's assignment, detailed above: "[On each assignment] all labor is quantified in words read or written, and in estimated time a student is expected to spend on the activity" (Inoue 2019, 130). There is a single standard of labor implicit across all three sites. How has this standard of labor been arrived at and by whom? How is this standard different from the static, single standard of quality that labor-based grading contracts are intended to challenge?

Unfortunately, this assessment practice seems to neglect important groups of students whose labor is not represented by this standard, including students who are physically and otherwise disabled and students who are twice (or more) marginalized, the implications of which I discuss in more detail below.[1]

Beyond the foundational assumption upon which labor-based contract grading rests—namely that labor is neutral—there are other assumptions that inform this assessment practice that are worth addressing. I want to spend some time unpacking the concept of "willingness" that is central at least to Inoue's version of labor-based grading contracts. I intend to complicate the assumption that a willingness to labor is enough to succeed within the labor-based grading contract ecology he describes.

While willingness may or may not be at the center of all labor-based grading contracts, it does seem to inform the very

---

1. While my focus is on students with disabilities, there is important work to be done on instructors with disabilities and how their intersecting identities influence students' responses to assessment practices, including grading contracts. Although not focused on assessment practices, see teacher-scholar Stephanie L. Kerschbaum's (2014) "On Rhetorical Agency and Disclosing Disability in Academic Writing," which explores her own journey of disclosure in academic life. Also see Kerschbaum, O'Shea, Price, and Salzer's (2017) "Disclosure and Accommodations for Faculty Members with Mental Health Disabilities," which reports on a national survey of faculty members with mental health issues and explores their experiences with requesting and accessing accommodations at their institutions. Finally, see Cruz Medina and Kenneth Walker's (2019) "Validating the Consequences of Social Justice Pedagogy: Explicit Values in Course-Based Grading Contracts" for a discussion of how students respond to grading contracts adopted by a visibly raced instructor, particularly when an instructor takes a "non-normative" approach to teaching.

concept of labor. Moreover, because Inoue's model has circulated so widely, it's worthwhile to unpack that concept and the assumptions therein. The very goal of Inoue's writing courses draws on this concept of willingness:

> The purpose of this writing course is to encourage students to engage in a willingness to labor in mindful and meaningful reading and writing practices that lead them toward an awareness of language (and perhaps its politics) in a compassionate and safe environment that makes the course's opportunities for learning and all grades attainable by all students, no matter where they come from or the version of English they use. (2019, 244)

The emphasis on what Inoue (2019, 25) calls "noncognitive dimensions of students' learning," the category into which willingness falls, underscores his commitment to more inclusive assessment practices, and these dimensions play a role in how students are evaluated. Inoue (2019, 247) explains further, "Thus the overarching goal of labor-based grading contract ecologies, for me, is to get students to practice a network of interlocking, noncognitive competencies (engagement, coping and resilience, and metacognition), which I think of as a willingness to labor." Inoue does acknowledge, however, that there may be "unforeseen problems and situations that come up in students' lives . . . that may keep a student from meeting the contract obligations, despite their willingness to" (2019, 140). Inoue (2019, 140) explains that for this very reason he includes a "*gimme*" clause in the contract, a one-time free pass, so to speak, for each student. The very need for this clause suggests that one's willingness to labor is not always accompanied by one's ability to do so. Inoue, thus, creates an opening for more exploration of this very concept of willingness, as well as the assumption that students' willingness is enough to succeed in their courses.

As much as labor-based grading contracts are intended to eradicate inequities and may do so when it comes to racial formations, when willingness is conflated with ability—with just one chance per semester to decouple the two—students with disabilities are at a disadvantage. Just because someone is willing does not mean they are able to labor or at least labor in the ways that are expected when a normative body and neurotypical mind are at the center of an assessment model.

In addition to the barriers for those with disabilities that this approach poses, it also creates barriers for those belonging to certain socioeconomic classes. Inoue addresses this in his book, but finds solace in the fact that labor-based contracts only *reflect* rather than *cause* certain inequities:

> The conditions that create such time constraints for many students come from larger structural forces in society, the rising costs of higher education, the reduction of Pell grants and other support for college, changing admission standards, increasing wealth gaps between the very rich and everyone else, the need for more students to work while going to school, among other factors. Labor-based grading contract ecologies do not create the disadvantages of limited time that many students face, but they do make this larger societal problem more present and obvious, which may fool some into believing it creates the problem. (2019, 222)

The distinction that Inoue seems to be making here—and perhaps why he is focused on racial formations and language rather than class—is that whereas assessment practices *create* racist structures these practices only make the larger societal problems surrounding class "more present and obvious." Even if the relationship is not a causal one, it seems important to address the issues that emerge when we broaden the scope of the discussion surrounding assessment and look at students' identities in more complex ways, including their socioeconomic class.

Ira Shor, a prominent voice in early discussions about grading contracts, has also expressed how societal forces, including class, have posed recent challenges for him and his students as compared to when he wrote *When Students Have Power* in 1996. In that book, he describes his grading contract approach, as well as the important work of the "After-Class Group," a cadre of students who would stay after class to help co-create the class curriculum. He explained, however, in a 2017 interview that

> conditions for teaching and learning, as well as for everyday life and raising families, deteriorated dramatically for me and for the working-class students at my college across the 45 years I have taught there. Students were paying higher tuition for lower quality education. Many were unable to afford tuition and had to drop out after the class began. It became harder and more hostile to be a teacher or a student—bridge tolls and mass transit rose in cost, as did textbooks and food in the cafeteria. Fewer students would stay with me after class for the very unique and useful After-Class Group I began and wrote about in *When Students Have Power*. I discovered that the ACG worked best with a minimum of 4 students and a maximum of 8, but fewer than 4 typically volunteered in recent years. Students had to leave class immediately to go to jobs, to families, or to prepare for tests in other classes. Critical-democratic teaching and learning became a class luxury harder to practice here as the income inequality gap kept widening. (12)

Shor's compelling description of the changes in the educational, economical, and personal landscapes of his students' lives remind us that while students may be willing to participate, time is a luxury that not all students have. Essentially, Shor is pointing out the privilege associated with even being able to undertake "critical-democratic teaching and learning." In doing so, Shor reminds us that decoupling the willingness to labor from labor itself is an important way to avoid punishing those whose socioeconomic class does not afford them the luxury of engaging in labor even if they possess the will. What emerges is the need to focus on more than language and race in our assessment practices.

Inoue (2019, 225–226) does address the multidimensional ways in which labor is treated in his class, which could be said to mitigate some of the issues I describe above. He notes how labor is separated out in the following ways:

> (1) the ideal labor time required for most students to succeed in a class, expressed by both the teacher and the student; (2) the actual time for individual students to do [*sic*] succeed in the class; (3) the estimated labor time for all work calculated and provided by the teacher; and (4) the time each student feels they have available to spend on this class in order to get what they want out of it, which may fluctuate week by week.

While this approach potentially offers more flexibility than is necessarily visible in Inoue's assignments that lay out for students how much time they should spend on each task, the labor-based grading contract remains problematic because of the normative, neurotypical student at its center. For example, there is still an ideal amount of labor that has been calculated around which these discussions take place. Moreover, I suspect that the ideal amount of labor indicated on each assignment (and each task within each assignment) may feel stable and static to students even if offered only as an estimate. In other words, while I appreciate the multidimensional way in which Inoue explores and discusses labor with his students, we are still dealing with a normative student and a normative sense of time. Therefore, these contracts don't address how time is less available to students in certain socioeconomic classes and how time and labor function differently for students with disabilities, including those who are neurodivergent, as discussed in more detail in the next chapter.

# 2

## Substituting One Standard for Another
*The Normative, Laboring Body at the Center of*
*Labor-Based Grading Contracts*

While intended to remove a single standard of quality from the center of traditional grading practices, labor-based contracts simply shift the focus of assessment from quality to labor with the former representing a White-supremacist form of violence against students and the latter representing a more democratized, inclusive, and equitable assessment practice. In doing so, however, one standard is simply substituted for another. This sort of substitution is especially dangerous because quantifiable information—the kind of information that is collected by students as they labor—gives the appearance of objectivity. Numbers carry with them a certain air of objectivity, yet we know that numbers are not inherently objective and don't tell any kind of story on their own. With its focus on quantitative measures—namely how much labor students undertake—this assessment practice actually obscures the single standard of labor upon which it depends, a standard that necessarily excludes the growing number of students in our classrooms for whom this standard is not a reality. While labor-based grading contracts make labor visible, these contracts, unfortunately, simultaneously obscure the problematic normative body and conception of labor at their center.

Disability studies offers useful ways for thinking about the role of the body in making meaning (Dolmage 2014; Rule 2017) even if the body is often erased from instructional materials such as writing textbooks (King 2019, 96–98). As such, I very much appreciate Inoue's emphasis on embodiment in his scholarship and research on assessment practices. In fact, Inoue has chosen the term "labor" precisely because he does not want to erase students' bodies: "Labor is a reference to doing things, to acting, to performing, to working in honorable, embodied ways" (Inoue 2019, 16). Yet, labor-based grading contracts appear to assume an able-bodied student, thereby placing at its center what disability studies scholar Rosemarie Garland-Thomson (1996) has called a "normate," a figure that exists in opposition to the disabled body. Inoue (2019, 77) seemingly has a normate body in mind when he imagines the body in labor:

> Labor requires a body in motion, even if the motions are small or slight. We speak through our bodies. Our lungs inhale air, chest and belly expand and relax, mouth opens and closes, lips and tongue dance together. Each time we speak, our bodies move in amazingly elaborate and coordinated ways, like a synchronized dance group, each dancer moving their part, forming a larger organism that produces something more than the sum of the individuals dancing. Our brains also expend a lot of energy doing the work of thinking and processing.

There are many students whose bodies are not reflected in this description, whose bodies struggle to—don't or can't—"move in coordinated ways." This certainly applies to students with physical disabilities, but neurodiverse students, and specifically autistic students, who are more often understood in terms of their neurodivergence rather than physical disabilities, often report difficulty controlling their bodies within the classroom setting and experience motor movement difference (McKee and Gomez 2020). In other words, these students must labor more than other students to even control their own bodies. The labor that students with disabilities expend is at the very least different—but also likely just plain more in terms of quantity—than is required by the imagined able-bodied student at the center of labor-based grading contracts.

Like many instructors, I have witnessed various forms of this labor first-hand. Paralyzed students in wheelchairs, for example, often must labor to even find a space in classrooms that are outfitted with cumbersome stationary furniture. Students who are blind, deaf, or hard of hearing will often use assistive technologies—tools or devices that help people with disabilities perform tasks more easily or with greater independence—which certainly have incredible benefits, but often increase the amount of labor that these students expend on any given task. This added labor involves grappling with the technology itself, which might include the extra steps of uploading or downloading information or files, dealing with the imperfections of technologies like text-to-speech software, and struggling with interfaces and software that prove incompatible with e-readers.

Because of the extra labor involved in simply moving through one's daily routine, those with disabilities also often experience what Annika Konrad (2021) calls "access fatigue" as people with disabilities are constantly trying to negotiate access to the "habits and structures that need to change to support more inclusive public life" (185). Maier et al. have described how exhausting this work is especially for "multiply marginalized" (2020) people:

> We must constantly educate others regarding "what it means
> to live as" trans and/or nonbinary people, as people of color,

as disabled persons. . . . You and we do not take our access to institutional resources for granted; we are all familiar with what it's like when we are barred from some of those resources. Part of our work, therefore, consists of self-creating access—whether in the form of collectively compelling our institutions to accommodate our bodyminds, or struggling to invent new minutes and hours to finish our tasks (perhaps forgoing sleep or other important sustainability services), or independently developing the knowledge or skill to forage for our own resources.

Konrad's concept of access fatigue provides a framework for understanding precisely what Maier et al. describe, namely the "societal conditions that pressure disabled people to rely on their own self—rather than all people and their complicit participation in systems of power that create inaccessible spaces" (Konrad 2021, 185). We can take a first step toward stemming the notion that disabled people are "independently responsible for access [and] we can relieve some of the pressure" (Konrad 2021, 197) by revisiting and revising the normate body and mind at the center of labor-based grading contracts.

As I will discuss in more detail below, it would seem that students who have any disability—including physical, developmental, neurological, sensory, or psychological—that affects how they labor are put at a disadvantage by labor-based grading contracts. Not only is an able-bodied and neurotypical student at the center of these contracts, but the specified amount of labor that students are asked to spend on assignments, as well as individual tasks within those assignments, is also created according to some single standard very much indebted to able-bodied labor practices.

Before going further, I must pause to address the importance of keeping in mind, as Stephanie L. Kerschbaum (2015) does, that "disability is not a static identity that is deter-mined *a priori* when students enter a classroom," but instead is "emerging, relational, and always-in-flux." As I discuss disability throughout this essay, I never intend to stabilize it, but rather to point out how attention to disability can result in important social change, including across institutions, such as the educational system that was founded on and contin-ues to function according to ableist norms and expectations (Dolmage 2017).

The ableist norm that labor-based grading contracts posit is concerning precisely because labor-based grading contracts are becoming an increasingly popular approach to assessment in postsecondary institutions. Because an able-bodied stan-dard is at the center of this assessment practice, this assessment practice will likely, in the end, reward students with those very bodies—or those closest to it—the same way that traditional quality-based assessments "mostly hel[p] those students in striking distance to the standards" (Inoue 2019, 215). These traditional assessment ecologies, which labor-based grading contracts are supposed to challenge, allow "those who already have the closest relation to the White, middle-class habitus of the standard to be rewarded, and gives them the biggest share of those rewards, which starts with grades" (Inoue 2019, 215). The same seems to be true if we shift from a racial context to a disability context. The students whose bodies are most like the normative body at the center of the labor-based con-tracts are most likely to be rewarded through this approach to assessment.

As we consider ways to recognize and work toward alle-viating the inequities in our assessment practices, we must, in the words of disability studies scholar Tara Wood (2017, 261), address how the education system allows these "normative assumptions to go unchecked."[2] While labor-based grading contracts potentially do important anti-racist work, their work toward inclusivity remains incomplete. Research continues to show that students with disabilities experience "psychological, behavioral, and academic challenges, similar to those commonly experienced by other marginalized groups that ultimately impact academic performance and success" (Bessaha et al. 2020). Moreover, when we talk about students with disabilities, we are talking about a significant portion of students, particularly if you incorporate those with anxiety and depression, as addressed in the next chapter. According to the US Department of Education's National Center for Education Statistics (2019), 19 percent of undergraduates in 2015–2016 reported having a disability. This percentage is almost twice as large as the statistic from three years prior—11 percent—reported by the US Department of Education.

But this number only counts the documented cases of students with disabilities, and we know that not all students

---

2.  Research and scholarship about students with disabilities in two-year and community colleges, in particular, have been lagging, a point Holly Hassel makes in "Research Gaps in Teaching English in the Two-Year College." Hassel notes that in the last thirty years *Teaching English in the Two-Year College* (TETYC) has published only five articles and one response on the subject. Yet, "students with disabilities who attend college are more than twice as likely to attend two-year or community colleges (44%) than four-year institutions (19%) as their peers without disabilities (21%)" (Madaus et al., 2021, 31). In March 2022, *TETYC* will be publishing a special issue on disability, accessibility, and teaching English in the two-year college that will be edited by Adam Hubrig. Perhaps the special issue will provide insights into the kinds of assessment practices that have been developed to include the number of students with disabilities at these institutions, inclusive assessment practices that can be adapted by all kinds of institutions. For an overview of trauma-informed writing pedagogy and how it can help create psychologically safer classrooms at two-year institutions and beyond, see Melissa Tayles's "Trauma-Informed Writing Pedagogy: Ways to Support Student Writers Affected by Trauma and Traumatic Stress."

with disabilities disclose their disabilities to their institutions (Low 1996; Prowse 2009). For example, 72 percent of students who transfer from two-year institutions to four-year institutions (Newman et al. 2011) don't disclose their disability. We also know that students belonging to certain racial and ethnic groups are less likely to disclose a disability (Bailey and Mobley 2019, 25). Additionally, as Pearson and Boskovich (2019) point out, "due to negative perception of disability," students with disabilities may choose to "assimilate in order to maintain a positive image and ensure smooth transaction with able-bodied individuals." In other words, the 19 percent statistic is likely significantly lower than the actual number of undergraduates with disabilities.

The stakes are high for students with disabilities, of whom only 34 percent are likely to graduate four-year institutions as compared to 51 percent of their able-bodied peers (Newman et al. 2011, xxvi). As such, it's important that our assessment practices, especially in first-year courses, position students with disabilities to succeed. When we think about how students who experience anxiety and depression might fare with labor-based grading contracts, the potentially deleterious effects become even clearer. These effects have the potential to be especially widespread as anxiety and depression are "the most common presenting concerns assessed by clinicians" in college and university counseling centers (Center for Collegiate Mental Health 2020, 19).

# 3

# Labor-Based Contract Grading and Students' Mental Health

As this chapter considers students' experiences with anxiety and depression, it's important to keep in mind the complex ways in which anxiety and disability interact for students. As Wood (2017, 270) points out, "The connections between disability and anxiety are complex and must be considered contextually. For some students, anxiety is their disability; for others, it might be a symptom; and for still others, it might just be anxiety (unrelated to a diagnosed disability)." While the scope of this essay doesn't allow for the integration of the voices of students with disabilities or case studies of specific students, both of which are paramount in scholarship within disability studies, it is useful to draw on the statistics that capture the widespread effect of anxiety and depression on students across the country.

Even prior to the COVID-19 pandemic, the numbers of students who reported experiencing anxiety and/or depression were staggering. According to the ACHA-National College Health Assessment II (2019), a national research survey of nearly seventy-four thousand students, sponsored by the American College Health Association, 88.1 percent of students reported feeling "overwhelmed by all [they] had to do" in the year leading up to the 2019 study. Additionally, 64.3 percent of students reported feeling "overwhelming anxiety" and 42.9 percent "felt so depressed that it was difficult to function."[3] The 2019 Annual Report of the Center for Collegiate Mental Health (2020, 19) shared similar findings, noting that 62.7 percent of the study's 82,685 respondents reported experiencing anxiety and depression, making these the most common concerns of students who visit college and university counseling centers. Additionally, the study (2020, 5) pointed out that "average rates of student self-reported anxiety and depression increased over the past eight years."[4]

Just as the pandemic exposed and increased racial disparities across the country, it also exposed and increased mental health issues, including anxiety and depression, among students. A national and equally diverse survey of thirty-three thousand college students was conducted during the pandemic.

---

3.    The data set from the study consists of 73,912 students from 140 institutions across the United States, including private and public institutions, as well as two- and four-year colleges. The racial makeup is important, too, because it suggests that these mental health issues cross racial boundaries. Just under 5 percent of respondents identified as Black or African American; 18.5 percent identified as Hispanic or Latino/a; 13.1 percent identified as Asian or Pacific Islander American Indian, Alaskan Gender Native or Native Hawaiian; 5.2 percent identified as Biracial or Multiracial; 2.6 identified as Other; and 64.7 percent of respondents identified as White. Even if we take the lowest statistic here—the 42.9 percent of students who "felt so depressed that it was difficult to function" or, we might say, labor—that is a very significant percentage of students from this diverse random sampling that are potentially disadvantaged by the standard of labor that informs labor-based grading contracts.

4.    The study includes a diverse sampling, as well, with 9.9 percent of respondents identifying as African American or Black; 0.5 percent as American Indian or Alaska Native; 8.8 percent identifying as Asian American/Asian; 9.3 percent identifying as Hispanic/Latino; 0.2 percent identifying as Native Hawaiian or Pacific Islander; 5.1 percent identifying as Multiracial; 64.5 percent identifying as White; and 1.6 percent self-identifying.

The study included institutions from across the country and was administered by researchers Daniel Eisenberg, Sarah Ketchen Lipson, and Justin Heinze. They reported that 83 percent of students described their mental or emotional difficulties as having "hurt [their] academic performance" within the past four weeks, and 60 percent of students reported feelings of loneliness and isolation (Eisenberg, Lipson, and Heinze 2020, 6). Significantly smaller studies (Son et al. 2020; Fruehwirth, Biswas, and Perreira 2021; Dartmouth College 2020) focusing on students' mental health both before and during the COVID-19 pandemic confirm the findings of these large, national studies.

While purely anecdotal, I have noticed a marked increase in accommodations for students, particularly for anxiety and/or depression, as self-disclosed by the individual students. While roughly 25 percent of students in my most recent courses had accommodations, prior to that, the number of students with accommodations hovered around 10 percent. Keep in mind, too, that I teach at a campus with 48 percent students of color and 51 percent first-generation college students, populations of students that are often underserved throughout their early academic careers and less likely to disclose their disabilities later because of the cultural stigma that might surround asking for help, the shame that goes along with doing so, and the lack of awareness that such services exist and are free of charge (Pellegrino, Sermons, and Shaver 2011; Hampton and Sharp 2013; Morgan et al. 2017; Bailey and Mobley 2019). In other words, as with the statistics on the number of undergraduate students with disabilities, we must always keep in mind that there are plenty of students who do not disclose their disabilities, including 72 percent of students who transfer from two-year institutions to four-year institutions (Newman et al. 2011), as noted above. As such, when we strive toward creating inclusive pedagogies, we must recognize that our efforts need to take into account the many students with disabilities that remain invisible for various reasons.

Experts have pointed out that just because the pandemic will come to an end does not mean that people will stop feeling its physical, emotional, and psychological effects. While it's impossible to predict all of these effects, psychologists have named the set of symptoms that many have already begun feeling since the onset of COVID-19 and will likely continue feeling for months and years to come. "Post-Covid stress disorder," "pandemic trauma," and "stress experience" are some of the terms being used to describe the PTSD-like symptoms that accompany both direct and indirect exposure to COVID-19 (Bridgland et al. 2021; Tucker and Czapla 2021). As such, it's important to create assessments that address the already significant and growing population of students who experience anxiety and depression. We do not want to put students experiencing anxiety and depression—whether long-term or temporarily—at a disadvantage by creating a standard of labor that excludes them.

The concerns I have raised regarding the exclusion of students with disabilities from labor-based contract grading schemas are not totally neglected by Inoue and others who champion labor-based grading contracts. In fact, as noted in the introduction, I decided to enter this conversation in part because Inoue seems open to recognizing ways to improve this assessment practice, an openness that is underscored by Chapter 6 of *Labor-Based Contract Grading*, which Inoue (2019, 18) uses to answer "fourteen questions concerning the use of labor-based grading contracts . . . gathered from various teachers and others from across the US and on the WPA-L [Writing Program Administrators' Listserv]."

In that chapter, Inoue addresses these and related issues outright. However, I think we can and must go even further as we imagine ways to make labor-based grading contracts more inclusive. For example, in response to a question about emotional labor that some students must endure, a question that seems to dovetail nicely with my present concern about students' experiences with anxiety and depression, Inoue (2019, 221) notes that "it is comforting for me to remember that while we can prepare for many possibilities in our classrooms, we cannot prepare for all of them, and while we can want to address issues around emotional labor and strain in our classrooms, issues we know exist, we may not always be able to know beforehand if those issues will arise in this particular class with these particular students." What I would like to suggest, however, is that in light of the widespread anxiety and depression that students have experienced and will likely continue to experience, we should not "wait-and-see then be-compassionate-and-let-go" (Inoue 2019, 221), but, instead, anticipate this and build it into our assessment practices. No one would argue that the "wait-and-see" approach is sufficient when it comes to antiracist pedagogies. Instructors, in other words, would never set aside an antiracist form of assessment or pedagogy simply because no students of color showed up in their class that semester. As Kerschbaum (2015) reminds us, "We need to imagine what happens when disabled students are in our classrooms, and this imagining needs to happen before someone actually discloses a disability. Whether disclosures happen or not, disability will always be part of classroom life everywhere."

To related questions about how disability might be addressed within the labor-based grading contract framework, Inoue (2019, 230) points out that a strength of these contracts is that they are "flexible enough to provide appropriate affordances for a range of learners," affordances that can be requested and applied through negotiation. Inoue specifically details how this flexibility can support students "with difficulties around executive functioning" (2019, 231–232) and students who must endure "emotional labor and strain in our classrooms" (2019, 221). While I appreciate the flexibility built into the contract, I would point out that this approach asks students to negotiate against a standard of labor that is inherently unfair and inequitable.

Moreover, an assessment that depends on students with disabilities to negotiate poses issues related to disclosure, whether students are invited to negotiate in private with the instructor or as part of a whole class contract negotiation. Many of the chapters in *Negotiating Disability: Disclosure and Higher Education*, an edited collection that focuses on what it means to disclose a disability within higher education, consider the complexities surrounding disclosure. Tonette S. Rocco and Joshua C. Collins, for example, consider how many students with disabilities struggle to disclose their disability for various reasons, including a lack of understanding and/or inability to articulate their accommodation needs, which may stem from a new diagnosis or a lack of adequate information from a campus counselor or advisor about both the disability and relevant accommodations (Rocco and Collins 2017, 336). As Rocco and Collins point out, "Without adequate knowledge and experience, articulating accommodation needs concisely and with assurance is difficult and can make a student appear incompetent and full of excuses for inadequate performance" (2017, 336), thereby reducing their credibility and the chances that an instructor will provide the requested accommodation.

Assessments like labor-based grading contracts that depend on learners' retroactive requests for accommodations rather than instructors' proactive attempts at inclusivity create a situation that disability justice advocate Mia Mingus (2011) has coined "forced intimacy" in which "disabled bodies must disclose their disability to able-bodied people in order to gain access to what is already accessible to normative bodies." Mingus describes these experiences as "exploitative, exhausting, and violating."

When asked to negotiate in front of a full class, students with disabilities who already believe that their "peers do not understand why [they] still need accommodations at the college level" (Timmerman and Mulvihill 2015, 1618) are potentially marginalized further. As I consider Inoue's weekly negotiations with the full class of students about "how much time realistically each student can commit to the class, and what that will mean in terms of meeting learning goals and the minimum requirements of the grading contract" (Inoue 2019, 226), I am reminded of Peter Elbow's (2006, 91) critique of Inoue's community-based grading contracts. Elbow points out that because the goal is to agree on a standard of writing, the minority viewpoints are necessarily erased. I have similar concerns, in addition to those about forced intimacy, mentioned above, regarding how students with disabilities might fare during these negotiations.

Still, these weekly negotiations do offer opportunities to discuss disability. Drawing on Amber R. Knight's scholarship, Pearson and Boskovich (2019) acknowledge the potential salutary effects of "ignit[ing] a conversation around disability as part of the everyday process" and "open[ing] up the possibilities of all bodies beginning to understand not only their role, but the importance of collective accountability, within the complex web of power and oppression that flourishes within an academic culture." I can, then, imagine ways in which making disability a part of class discussions could be important and useful, but it would be crucial for instructors to educate themselves on how to create productive conversations surrounding disability that don't further marginalize already marginalized students. There are any number of ways that instructors might create a space that is conducive to these conversations, including creating syllabi and other course documents that underscore our "collective accountability" (Pearson and Boskovich 2019) by highlighting resources for students with disabilities and refraining from including ableist language; incorporating texts into one's courses that can be productively read through a disability studies lens; assigning texts by authors with disabilities; and refraining from putting students with disabilities in the position of being "the voice of disability" (Breneman et al. 2017, 349) during class discussions.

Working against further marginalizing already marginalized students also, of course, means thinking about accessibility. Some labor-based grading contracts may already incorporate attention to the needs of students with disabilities through universal design for learning (UDL) principles. Inoue, for example, readily acknowledges the importance of addressing disability in his assessments even if he remains focused primarily on racial formations and language diversity. Inoue explains that he has created his labor-based grading contracts with UDL principles in mind, noting that these contracts encourage teachers and students to consider "what kinds of reasonable accommodations can the course make for those who feel they will have trouble meeting the labor demands of the class while still maintaining the expectations of the course" (2019, 229). Moreover, I suspect that many grading contracts have a sort of safety valve like Inoue's *gimme* that students with disabilities might take advantage of, too. As noted above, this "plea or gimme clause," explains Inoue (2019, 140), is used "to address these unexpected issues that affect their abilities to do the labor in the manner expected in the class. So this clause allows anyone to escape the penalty for such things, but only once in the quarter or semester." Because of the limited scope of this clause, though, it doesn't adequately address even a temporary disability that a student might experience during the course of a semester.

Despite being well-intentioned, this kind of retrofitting is problematic across educational institutions, which is why scholars in disability studies have called for less retrofitting and more proactive approaches to disability. Jay Dolmage (2006, 20) explains that to retrofit "is to add a component or accessory to something that has already been manufactured or built. This retrofit does not necessarily make the product function, does not necessarily fix a faulty product, but it acts as a sort of correction." As Ella R. Browning (2014, 100) explains, though, "Rather than simply retrofitting our universities, our classroom spaces, and our pedagogies, we must actively integrate disability, in thoughtful and critical ways, into all aspects of our teaching." Lewiecki-Wilson and Brueggemann (2008) similarly describe the need to "rebuild" rather than "retrofit" as a way of proactively anticipating and addressing potential biases in one's teaching methods.

Inoue is undoubtedly right that we cannot prepare for every possible issue that may arise in our classrooms. Still, we can and should call out nonracially motivated forms of bias and injustice—in addition to racially and linguistically motivated forms—and proactively, rather than retroactively, work toward more inclusive assessments that need not be negotiated by students who are disadvantaged by the normative body and standard of labor, as well as the neurotypical student, at the center of an assessment model. That is not to say we must choose antiracist pedagogies *or* pedagogies that are more inclusive of students with disabilities, and in no way do I mean to pit one against the other. In fact, because both perspectives are intended to increase inclusivity, these perspectives can enrich one another. As instructors create their syllabi, assignments, and assessments, thinking about all of these aspects of their courses through both an antiracist perspective as well as a disability studies perspective is an important step toward more thoroughly inclusive teaching and assessment practices.

# 4

# Labor-Based Contract Grading and Students' Intersectional Identities

Labor-based grading contracts clearly address students' intersectional identities. Inoue's contracts and similar contracts, in fact, set out to directly address the raciolinguistic aspects of students' identities. Still, there are ways to expand the scope of labor-based grading contracts to put fewer students at a disadvantage, and doing so involves addressing intersectionality more comprehensively. I use the term "intersectionality" in the way it was introduced by Kimberlé Crenshaw roughly thirty years ago to expose how certain people are subject to multiple forms of inequality based on their multiple identity positions. In a feature article by Katy Steinmetz (2020), Crenshaw explains the concept of intersectionality after decades of "distortion," which has cast it as "identity politics on steroids." Crenshaw notes that intersectionality is a useful term because "we tend to talk about race inequality as separate from inequality based on gender, class, sexuality or immigrant status. What's often missing is how some people are subject to all of these, and the experience is not just the sum of its parts."

While labor-based grading contracts are intended to support non-White students in particular, these students who are twice (or more) marginalized because of their intersecting identities would not experience the same advantages. With the normative body at the center of labor-based grading contracts, for example, Black students who are disabled are disadvantaged in ways that able-bodied Black students potentially are not. Research shows, however, that "Black people experienced higher odds of disability across the adult lifespan compared with white people" (Nuru-Jeter et al. 2011, 834) even though students of color who are disabled are less likely to be screened and identified as having disabilities than their white classmates (Morgan et al. 2017). As Wendy S. Harbour et al. (2017, 158) note, several studies (Petersen 2009; Banks and Hughes 2013; and Banks 2014) over the last ten years have shown that "African American college students with disabilities wrestle with identities as both African Americans and people with disabilities." Writing studies has an opportunity here to take the lead alongside critical race, feminist, disability studies scholars, and others who recognize the importance of attending to intersectionality in the classroom. Moreover, it is crucial to work against the tendency in disability studies to erase Black bodies and the tendency in Black studies to erase disabled bodies (Bailey and Mobley 2019). We can, in other words, develop assessments that recognize and value students' multiple identities.

Assessment practices that incorporate attention to intersectionality have been especially helpful to Kathleen Kryger and Griffin X. Zimmerman (2020), who have used labor-based grading contracts as a basis from which to

> develop an intersectional model of writing assessment [that] makes institutional space for a few key conversations: (a) cripping time in our grading systems and program policies so that neurodivergent conceptions of time, effort, and presence can be adequately accounted for; (b) flexible pedagogies for various modes and ways of learning and being; and (c) the

denaturalization of White supremacy, especially within linguistic ideologies.

Kryger and Zimmerman's approach recognizes the importance
of denaturalizing White supremacy while also acknowledging
that assessment practices are often biased in other ways that need
to be addressed. With their attention to nonnormative conceptions of time and effort, as well as their emphasis on flexibility,
all of which complement the antiracist aspect of their assessment
practice, they suggest productive avenues for assessment.

Ira Shor et al.'s (2017) description above about how
"critical-democratic teaching and learning became a class luxury
harder to practice" also suggests a path forward that involves
attending not only to race, but to class, in our assessments.
Underscoring how socioeconomic class intersects with race and
(dis)ability, Emily Krebs (2019) explains how this affects the
very students who get accommodations:

> While some college students and/or their families can afford
> testing, others altogether cannot [so they cannot get accom-
> modations]. This means that disabled students from low-
> income backgrounds are less likely to succeed than their
> wealthy peers, adding a layer of difficulty to the already dismal
> numbers of students with disabilities finishing baccalaureate
> degrees. Furthermore, being from a lower-class background
> means that poor students with disabilities are more likely to
> be seen as "moochers" on the system than their wealthy peers,
> thus making them more susceptible to scrutiny when they
> receive accommodations.

Having considered the "poor medical care for racial minorities," the "racial biases in diagnostic criteria," and the "fears of
medical care," Krebs ultimately concludes that the process of
securing documentation for disability accommodations "is an
unintentionally-racist requirement" (n.p.). Recognizing that the

very process by which students secure accommodations for their disabilities is inherently—albeit unintentionally—racist should compel us to expand the focus of our assessments to address inequities that extend beyond race but also often include it.

M. Remi Yergeau, a self-identified autistic academic, has commented, too, on the importance of addressing intersectionality noting, for example, "the exclusion of autistic people of color from the broadest reaches of both nonautistic and autistic-led advocacy," as well as the privilege Yergeau is afforded because of their subject positions. In the introduction to their award-winning book, *Authoring Autism*, Yergeau (2018, 5) explains:

> As a white autistic who has attained considerable education—I am a professor who can, even if only infrequently, access reliable speech—I write this book with great trepidation, and resignation, that autism politics routinely reward those who are multiply privileged. The logics of ableism are intertwined with the logics of racism, classism, and heterosexism. And while autism unto itself reduces my ethos as an interlocutor, whiteness, class, and speech configure my claims to personhood very differently than those who occupy more marginal positions.

Considering Yergeau's more general argument for recognizing intersectionality alongside Kryger and Zimmerman's and Krebs's more specific arguments about the barriers that stand in the way of multiply marginalized students reveals the complexity of the situation. When taken together, these arguments highlight how intertwined subject positions truly are, thereby suggesting that students would benefit from more inclusive assessments that address the intersection of race with other identities, including socioeconomic class and (dis)ability.

When we understand the importance of attending to intersectionality in its most encompassing sense, grading contracts that put a neurotypical, normative able-bodied student at their center ultimately prove to be an unintentionally ableist form of assessment. Recognizing that his students may, in fact, labor differently, Inoue explains that just "because it is unrealistic to ask everyone to perform the same ideal labor in the same ways doesn't mean we cannot articulate what we understand at the moment to be ideal labor as a kind of shore marker or buoy to help give reference to those in the ecology." However, when the referent is an able-bodied, neurotypical student, it does become a problem for all students the same way that racist assessment practices are a problem for all students and not just those in racial minorities. Moreover, when we consider how gender and sexual orientation (Miller, Wynn, and Webb 2017) as well as ethnicity and citizenship status (Cedillo 2020) intersect with the identities already discussed, the systems of structural discrimination necessarily expand.

Considering the intersectionality of race and class when creating assessments seems especially important because students' levels of preparedness are often tied to both. Students who come from high schools in underserved areas that don't supply students with the most basic tools of education are likely to struggle in ways that their richer, White peers do not when they get to college. Of course, the very concept of preparedness is complex, as Inoue (2019, 28) points out while clarifying his use of the term: "When I say 'most prepared,' I really mean the most prepared to use the dominant, White discourse that the classroom in question rewards. Many students who come to us with other Englishes have been prepared, only prepared in linguistically other ways." But I think there is more to it than simply the difference in racial formations. As I suggest above, socioeconomic class seems to also play a role in how preparedness is understood and unfolds in the classroom.

Moreover, while labor-based contract grading is posited as an antidote to "conventionally graded ecologies" (Inoue 2019, 137) where quality reigns, the examples that Inoue includes in *Labor-Based Grading Contracts* seem to undercut his own argument, which is why I suspect we should be looking at other aspects of students' identities to help us create more inclusive forms of assessment that can more consistently meet the goals of labor-based grading contracts. Inoue explains (2019, 138) that "the difference in labor-based contracts is in the reasonable chances of all students—not some of them, not the 'most prepared' among them, but all of them—to get any grade possible, including the highest." The examples and data he includes about the effectiveness of labor-based grading contracts, which I address in later chapters in more detail, show that students of color are laboring more than their White peers but often still ending up in the lower tiers when his students are separated out by their final grades (2019, 251–252). Because this is discussed in more detail in the following chapter, I'll simply note here that while labor-based contract grading is supposed to benefit those very students who might traditionally be categorized as underprepared, labor-based grading contracts, at least as reported by Inoue, seem to cause these students to labor more without awarding them the benefit of higher grades. Yet, in this assessment ecology there is supposed to be a direct correlation between the amount of labor expended and a student's final grade: "Final grades produced in labor-based grading contract ecologies equate quite directly to the amount and nature of labor expended in the course" (Inoue 2019, 155). This leads me to wonder whether socioeconomic and/or other intersectional identities are at play and whether assessment practices that take into consideration students' multiple identities might better achieve the goals Inoue lays out.

A more intersectional approach to assessment might provide the means to address the labor differential between the White students and students of color in Inoue's classes. Moreover, a more consistent treatment of labor as separate from quality might also be beneficial. Inoue reports that he regularly talks to his students about producing more labor. Still, these conversations sound like conversations about quality that are masquerading as conversations about labor. Inoue explains (2019, 202): "Often I'm telling students something like, 'if the instructions say that you should spend twenty-five to thirty minutes, factor a bit more time for yourself, maybe forty-five minutes. It appears you may need some extra time to produce the kind of material that will help you in the class.'" On the surface, Inoue is suggesting that the student undertake more labor, but note how that labor is connected to quality. The word "quality" is not used here, but if we home in on the phrase "extra time to produce the kind of material that will help you" we can infer that the students' labor is producing low quality material that could benefit from and become higher quality with some additional labor. In other words, quality (although not called such) seems to still play a role in this assessment practice, at least as this common interaction is represented. The issue, then, as I see it, is twofold: First, we must be aware that even with the best intentions, labor-based grading contracts are not necessarily rewarding extra labor, extra labor that often comes from students whose race and class (and perhaps other subject positions) put them at a disadvantage upon entering college. Second, labor-based grading contracts can easily revert to instruments that measure quality, which is the very measurement they seek to avoid.

This twofold issue makes the kinds of conversations that Kryger and Zimmerman (2020) call for that much more urgent. As they point out, we must create institutional spaces for conversations that lead to grading systems and program policies that account for neurodivergent conceptions of time and labor, as well as pedagogies that recognize and include the widest possible range of modes of learning and of being.

# 5

## The Effectiveness of Labor-Based
## Grading Contracts

Studying the effectiveness of one's assessment practices is integral to building and maintaining strong pedagogies. When exploring the effectiveness of labor-based contract grading, as the studies summarized below do, you will notice that none looks at this form of assessment through a disability lens.

It is widely accepted that assessment work is best done locally, which aligns with Inoue's overall assessment ecology:

> If literacies are bound up not just with communication but with our identities and the social formations that people find affinity with, if literacy is bound up with how we understand and make our worlds, then a world with literacy classrooms that use singular standards to determine progress and grades of locally diverse students, a world that holds every student in the classroom to the same standard regardless of who they are or where they came from or what they hope for in their lives, is a world that tacitly provides and validates the logics of White supremacy. (Inoue 2019, 306)

Inoue is, of course, right that using "singular standards to determine progress and grades of locally diverse students" is problematic. Similarly, we shouldn't try to generalize about the effectiveness of labor-based grading contracts by drawing on the findings from the few studies we have from local classroom contexts that are not our own. Despite the increased attention to and adoption of grading contracts, particularly in the last two years, it's probably too early to expect a groundswell of empirical data surrounding the use of grading contracts. We can, however, look to the handful of small studies that have been published to see how this form of assessment has fared over the years, as well as to consider whether any of these approaches to contract grading hold promise for the future. This chapter offers a brief review of those studies in chronological order. As this chapter makes clear, relatively few studies have been conducted on grading contracts. Additional research, including that attuned to disability, seems crucial.

The effectiveness of grading contracts in writing classrooms has been studied from a range of perspectives and myriad approaches. Overall, though, there is very little research on the subject. The dearth of research through 2006 led William H. Thelin and Cathy Spidell (2006, 36) to develop a study to "learn more about how students experience grading contracts." The grading contract system that Spidell used in her writing classroom, the site of the study, was indebted to both Peter Elbow's and Ira Shor's philosophies, for whom grading contracts represented an escape from grading and a crucial element of a critical democratic classroom, respectively. Thelin and Spidell (2006, 37) explain, "We designed our study, then, to bring student voices into the conversation . . . we also desired student input into the efficacy of the contract system, its fairness, its clarity, and its relevance to their educational background and goals." Thelin and Spidell used "purposeful sampling as a means to balance [the] student sample to align ethnically with classroom demographics" (39) and collected feedback throughout the semester from thirty-eight participating students at a midwestern four-year university with primarily middle-class and working-class students. "The patterns we uncovered from the data revealed considerable resistance" (2006, 40), explain Thelin and Spidell.

The resistance they describe was a result of various factors including students' difficulty "letting go of previous educational conditioning, much of which had disempowered them," as well as students' sense that grading contracts made the course more and unnecessarily difficult. They concluded that the implementation of the contracts into Spidell's classroom simply had not "done enough to change the educational atmosphere" (Thelin and Spidell 2006, 40). Thelin and Spidell (2006, 40) ultimately call for grading contracts "to be contextualized within a democratic, critical classroom, as advocated by Shor" and conclude their piece with a sort of warning: "A system of evaluation pretending to be anything but evaluative will cause both student suspicion and resentment" (55). The concerns that I have raised thus far about labor-based grading contracts are very much along these lines—labor-based grading contracts create a system of evaluation based on a standard (of labor) while pretending as if no standard exists.

Thelin and Spidell's study also raises another relevant issue regarding the relationship between effectiveness and student resistance. Student resistance, as Cruz Medina and Kenneth Walker (2018) remind us, does not necessarily mean that contract grading is not effective: "Rather than viewing student resistance to grading contracts negatively, critical pedagogy asserts that student resistance is a site to begin an inquiry into the ways in which students have internalized the dominant cultural narratives of grades, technologies, and instructors" (52). While not all instructors who use grading contracts are doing so within a critical pedagogy framework, it is useful to keep in mind the temptation to see student resistance as a vote against contract grading. Of course, the question becomes whether critical pedagogy is sustainable in a classroom in which an instructor compels students to engage in the work of negotiating grading contracts.

Glenda Potts (2010) describes her experience with similarly resistant students over the course of a year, from the summer of 2007 to the summer of 2008 at J. Sargeant Reynolds Community College in Richmond, Virginia. Potts conducted the study across nine English classes with a total of 188 students. Students were from composition classes, an introductory American literature class, and introductory creative writing classes. Potts notes that while "classic contract grading ordinarily features a written contract between instructor and student," she, instead, "adopted the 'blanket' contract format, whereby the instructor sets out the tasks that the student must complete in order to receive each letter grade, and the student complies according to the grade he or she wishes to receive" (2010, 31). Unlike the other studies described in this chapter, Potts took a comparative approach, keeping track of traditional grades (A–F), as well as the contract grades (accept/revise) that students earned throughout the semester. Potts (2010) explains that "Out of 188 students, 30 of the final grades awarded using the contract grading system differed slightly from those that would have been awarded in a traditional holistic system" with eleven of the thirty students receiving a C rather than an A or B "because they did not elect to complete an additional essay in order to receive the higher grade" (35). Interested in students' experiences of contract grading, Potts surveyed her students, and noted that "a significant number of A and B+ students did not like—in fact, despised—this grading system" (37). She explains further, "During the first semester the contract grading system was used, more than 80 percent of the higher achieving students hated it. In response to some of the reactions . . . in subsequent semesters I more thoroughly explained contract grading. Subsequent semesters showed a much higher level of acceptance by the A level students" (37). Despite students' mixed reactions, Potts reports that there were significant benefits associated with this assessment practice for her as an instructor. Grading, for example, proved less stressful and time-consuming and allowed her to appreciate and enjoy her students' writing in new ways.

The first study of its kind to consider the relationship between racial formations and the effectiveness of labor-based grading contracts is Inoue's 2009–2010 study of 432 students' experiences with contract grading in Fresno State's first-year writing program. The contracts in that program were based on Ira Shor (1996) and Jane Danielewicz and Peter Elbow's (2009) models, both of which "limit the teacher's power over student writing" (Inoue 2012, 83) and "pay little attention to the quality of writing" (83). Collecting data from anonymous exit surveys, final portfolio ratings, and course grade distributions, Inoue (2012) concludes that "the effectiveness of grading contracts in classrooms is unevenly distributed among racial formations and it sheds light on potential biases within Fresno State's grading contract approach" (93–94). The grading contracts benefited Asian Pacific Islanders the most and were just "somewhat effective" for African American students who "had more difficulty meeting all the contract obligations. The quantity of work expected in contracts appeared to be more difficult to complete for more African American students than any other racial formation," explains Inoue (93). Because of this, "African Americans' grade distributions achieve fewer 'As' and 'Bs' than any other group in both years" (89). These findings about

African American students are consistent with the data Inoue shares in *Labor-Based Grading Contracts*, although there is an important difference worth highlighting. While I will discuss this difference in more detail below, it is worth pointing out that whereas there seems to be a direct correlation in this study with the amount of labor put forth by African American students and the grades they received, the African American students that are represented in the classroom data Inoue shares in *Labor-Based Grading Contracts* labored *more* than their White peers but still ended up in the middle or bottom tier of the three-tiered class when it came to their final grades (155–156).

Like Inoue, Nayelee Uzan Villanueva (2014) took a multi-dimensional approach to evaluating the effectiveness of grading contracts. The study considers the impact of grading contracts on nine students in a basic writing course at an unnamed open enrollment state college in the southwest United States during the 2013 fall semester. Drawing on students' essays, interviews, reflection letters, and online negotiation dialogue, the study explored the "impacts of grade contracts on students' writing, motivation for writing, revision practices, authorship and expectations of a Basic Writing composition course" (26). Villanueva found that "by using a grade contract, students demonstrated higher levels of revision practices as well as levels of frequency" (iv). Villanueva explains further, "The results indicated that students perceived an increase in motivation as well as an increased sense of authorship. By engaging in a negotiation protocol, students perceived a higher level of control over their learning and role in the course" (iv).

Also studying so-called basic writers, Blackstock and Exton (2014, 280) similarly report the salutary effects of grading contracts at regional campuses of Utah State University. The students participating in the study ranged in age from twenty-five to fifty, were mostly first-generation Native American college students, and were working or raising children or grandchildren while attending college. Blackstock and Exton further explain that their students "largely fit the profile of basic writers" in that their "nontraditional students either never achieved writing proficiency in the public schools, for whatever reason, or have been out of school so long that they have lost whatever proficiency they might once have attained" (280–281). Ultimately, they concluded that for "students lacking in self-assurance or adequate preparation, the use of grading contracts can provide those students with space to grow in confidence, skill, and perhaps even love of writing" (290).

Less interested in students' self-efficacy and more interested in using grading contracts to increase student engagement and comprehension, Lisa M. Litterio (2016) conducted a 2014 study in a technical writing class. Litterio explains, "I wanted to experiment with contract grading to determine if students had more involvement in the grading process and more of an understanding of principles discussed in technical writing, such as usability and document design." Contrary to Villanueva's findings detailed above, Litterio found that "although students perceive more involvement in the grading process, they resist participation in crafting criteria as a class and prefer traditional grading methods by an 'expert,' considering it a normative part of the grading process."

While some of the research above addresses students' emotional and affective responses to contract grading, in their study of first-year writing students at the "most racially-diverse four-year institution in their state," Joyce O. Inman and Rebecca A. Powell (2018, 32) discovered that the affective work of grades needed to be foregrounded. They point to the dissonance that their study produced in many students: "the dissonance between appreciating the learning from a process made possible by the absence of grades and yearning for that same grade" (40). Inman and Powell conclude that "we must conduct more research on how and why students and instructors are so bound to grades and address this dissonance in our classrooms and our institutions" (49).

The studies briefly summarized above suggest that students' responses to and experiences with contract grading are mixed, which again supports the need for more research in this area—not to necessarily come to a single, unified judgment of the effectiveness of contract grading, but to understand it better as an assessment practice. Most striking, though, when we consider the effectiveness of labor-based grading contracts are the honest evaluations that Inoue offers of his own labor-based contract grading approach that, by his own admission, has yet to stem the racial inequities perpetuated by traditional grading systems.

I will focus on Inoue's discussion of the effectiveness of his labor-based grading contracts in two sites: "Grading Contracts: Assessing Their Effectiveness on Different Racial Formations" (2012) and *Labor-Based Grading Contracts* (2019). In both of these publications, Inoue raises concerns about the effectiveness of this form of assessment particularly for students of color. In his 2009–2010 study of first-year writing students at Fresno State, discussed above, the contracts proved just "somewhat effective" for African American students who Inoue notes (2012, 92) "had more difficulty meeting all the contract obligations. The quantity of work expected in contracts appeared to be more difficult to complete for more African American students than any other racial formation," explains Inoue (93). Because of this, "the African American grade distributions achieve fewer 'As' and 'Bs' than any other group in both years" (89). The study confirmed, at least, that the amount of labor that students did in the course was, in fact, reflected in their final grade, as is the goal of the labor-based contract approach: "Final grades produced in labor-based grading contract ecologies equate quite directly to the amount and nature of labor expended in the course" (Inoue 2019, 155).

Students of color fared similarly in terms of final grades in one of the courses Inoue (2019, 160) describes in *Labor-Based Grading Contracts*: "All three of the lowest grades in the course were given to students of color, the two Black students and a Latino." However, Inoue points out in that book that students of color typically labor more than their White peers in his classes. When Inoue (2019, 251) looks at what he calls "a typical distribution of grades and labor in my first-year writing courses," he concedes that "students of color do more labor, and are engaged at the same rates as their White peers" (251) but "that most of the students of color in this sample were in the middle and bottom groups" (251) of the three-tier system Inoue creates for final grades.

As far as I can tell, the labor-based contract ecology actually seems to disadvantage students of color, according to Inoue's data. Unlike the direct connection in his earlier study between the labor put into the course by students of color and their final grades, in this data set students of color labor more overall than their White classmates. Inoue explains that in a typical sample of fourteen students, students of color recorded "an average of almost 2 hours more labor each week" than his White students (251). These students aren't receiving the "bump" that Inoue's "immigrant students" receive (2019, 31) because they don't end up in the top tier of the class. Students of color, in other words, are doing more labor than their White classmates, but not being rewarded for it. This raises the question of why that extra labor is necessary. Perhaps these students aren't as prepared as their White peers, but if there is no White dominant standard at the center of labor-based contract assessments (according to which their preparedness would be judged) then we would expect a different outcome. Unless, of course, the issue is socioeconomics or some other aspect of students' identity and not the racial formation that is putting these students at a disadvantage.

Inoue offers additional details about this specific class: "One student, a Black male, did drop the course in the first few weeks of the class, and he seemed clearly to have other priorities in his life that kept him from doing the labor of the class and attending the class regularly. The other Black male in the classroom . . . who finished the course with a 2.1 [GPA], but did not complete a labor log, also had other priorities or issues in his life that kept him from doing more labor in the course." Ultimately Inoue (2019) concedes that "it is clear that even my example classroom above is no exception to this racializing of failure. . . . I cannot help but be concerned about the pattern in these two Black males, something our labor-based contract ecology clearly wasn't able to change, although one technically passed the course" (160).

I appreciate Inoue's willingness to address the shortcomings of this antiracist assessment practice, but I remain concerned because it is unclear what is separating labor-based contract grading from conventional grading ecologies wherein instructors "are asking for quality, but what that means in reality for many students of color and multilingual students is more time than their White, middle-class peers" (Inoue 2019, 222). Students of color are supposed to benefit from these contracts, but the data Inoue provides don't bear that out as students of color are doing roughly two more hours of labor per week than their White classmates but not earning anything in return for that labor, a point that Shane Wood (2020) has commented upon as well. While more research is certainly necessary, this emerging trend seems to support the need for a more comprehensive and intersectional approach to inclusivity in grading practices so that assessment practices are broad enough to address more than students' racial formations and linguistic diversity.

While we certainly need more studies of contract grading generally, and labor-based contract grading specifically, the data Inoue presents suggest that the philosophy that informs labor-based grading contracts overestimates the equalizing power of labor and underestimates the importance of intersectionality. Notice, for example, that Inoue describes the Black male who failed to finish the course as someone who "had other priorities or issues in his life that kept him from doing more labor in the course." While Inoue puts "the willingness to labor" at the center of his classes, we are reminded here again of the need to decouple willingness from ability to labor. I am not talking about some standard of academic ability, but rather the ability to commit a certain amount of time to a task. This student may have had the willingness, but to have the time to labor is a luxury that it sounds like he did not have.

Research on the effectiveness of labor-based grading contracts specifically, which I am calling for, could come from the institutions around the country (e.g., Langston University, University of Connecticut, Texas A&M University-San Antonio, Western Washington University, Humboldt University) where first-year writing programs and learning communities have adopted labor-based contract grading, many following the strictly labor-based model that Inoue describes, as opposed to a hybrid model that considers both labor and quality, such as that preferred by Jane Danielewicz and Peter Elbow (2009). These and other institutions that are using labor-based contract grading are important sites where research can be conducted to help us more fully understand the effectiveness of labor-based grading contracts in comparison to, as well as separate from, other grading approaches. Cowan (2020) agrees:

> As a field, composition could use more comparative, large-scale studies of grading contracts. Most scholarship on grading contracts in composition focuses on individual case studies of particular contract implementations along with the occasional survey of students in those classes. This information is useful for instructors developing their own grading contracts, but it does not reveal much about how grading contracts impact students academically or emotionally compared to other grading schemes.

Collecting data through large-scale studies will be an important step toward not just understanding the intellectual and affective implications of grading contracts for students (and teachers) but developing more inclusive kinds of grading contracts moving forward, the subject of the final chapter.

# 6

# Forging Ahead

*Outcomes [as opposed to course goals] ignore the students in front of us in favor of an idea of them and an idea of what that fictional group should learn, which of course may be based on teachers' senses of their past students. Thus, outcomes are a reification of learning that are created in part from a reification of future students.*

— Asao Inoue, *Labor-Based Grading Contracts*

*The stakes for identifying as disabled, or acknowledging a compromised relationship to labor and the ability to generate capital, is often not a viable option for most Black people. Stigma further complicates acknowledging disability, as it places an already precarious self at further risk of marginalization and vulnerability to state and medical violence, incarceration, and economic exploitation.*

— Moya Bailey and Izetta Autumn Mobley, "Work in the Intersections: A Black Feminist Disability Framework"

I juxtapose the epigraphs above in order to suggest where I think we can go from here. In the first epigraph, Inoue underscores the importance of basing assessment practices on the students "in front of us" rather than "a fictional group." My concern with the student at the center of labor-based grading contracts, though, is that this student is somewhat of a fiction; an idealized, able-bodied, neurotypical student. As important as it is to develop antiracist assessment practices, the second epigraph reminds us that we must not neglect other biases and inequities that intersect with racial biases and have the potential to seep into our assessment practices. We are also reminded of how high the stakes are for some students to acknowledge their intersectional identities, which raises the stakes for us as educators as we develop assessment practices that don't inherently disadvantage these students. With these epigraphs in mind, as well as Brueggeman's (2001, 795) point, quoted at the start of this essay, that "disability enables insight—critical, experiential, cognitive, sensory, and pedagogical insight," I suggest some next steps in the ongoing process of creating more inclusive assessments.

## ENGAGEMENT-BASED GRADING CONTRACTS

As I have discussed throughout, labor-based grading contracts seem to substitute one static standard for another. Built around a normative conception of labor, these contracts are potentially harmful to students with disabilities whose labor practices are not taken into consideration. Shifting the focus from labor to engagement might be preferable because it is more flexible than labor. Rather than instantiating a single standard, what I am calling "engagement-based grading contracts" offer a range of ways that students might engage with the course. Instead of being given a series of assignments and an estimated amount of time to spend on each assignment, students choose their forms of engagement and are assessed on those. Forms of engagement might include discussion board posts, oral participation in discussions, simulations (Rule 2017), collaborative note-taking (Hitt 2021), and a choice between alphabetic and multimodal responses to assignments. The engagement-based grading contracts I am proposing recognize the different ways students engage, as well as the different ways they create knowledge, a point that Brueggemann et al. (2001, 380) make in their call for supplementing writing-centered instruction in writing classrooms:

> Everyone can benefit from occasionally using nonwriting strategies to alter perspectives and create the intellectual distance needed for sophisticated revising. The system needs to change not because some people are labeled LD [learning disabled] but in spite of it. Those called "normal" also learn along a continuum of difference and would be better challenged if classrooms became more interactive, student-centered, multimodal, and collaborative. . . . When we expect all students—and ourselves—to think in oral, visual, and kinesthetic arenas, in addition to the ones that privilege written words, we learn from those who were previously excluded. . . . Being asked to conceptualize a project from a different perspective can trigger new insights for all writers, helping us generate connections we might not have made in word-locked prose.

The point Brueggemann et al. make, of course, is that all students benefit from the kind of flexible and interactive learning environment she describes, the very kind of environment that engagement-based grading contracts would cultivate. A more subtle point in this passage, and one Brueggeman has made elsewhere, is that seeing education through a disability studies lens can shed light on aspects of systems that otherwise remain unquestioned. In doing so, disability studies can help us reshape our pedagogical practices, including our assessment practices, so that they are more inclusive of the range of students, bodies, and minds that enter our classrooms. This emphasis on inclusivity is precisely what Allison Harper Hitt (2021) describes when she calls for "moving away from a diagnostic model of deficit and individual accommodations, and instead creating multiple access points for student engagement and emphasizing that diverse forms of meaning-making are assets" (86). Engagement-based grading contracts provide these access points and value the range of ways that students make meaning.

Following the lead of labor-based grading contracts, engagement-based grading contracts still bracket quality but do not rely on a single standard of labor that is not realistic for an increasing number of students. Engagement-based grading contracts, unlike Mathew Gomes's emphasis on "participation labor" in his labor-based grading contracts, as described in his co-authored piece with three students, remove the focus on labor altogether—and the normative conception of time that accompanies it—to create a more inclusive assessment practice (Gomes et al. 2020). Gomes's contract, which allows for "multiple forms of participation labor" in order to "contribute to the equity of courses using grading contracts" (n.p.) certainly makes his approach more inclusive than traditional labor-based grading contracts. However, while Gomes has removed a single, normative standard of participation from his assessment, labor, itself, as the larger category, still remains intact. This approach is reminiscent of Inoue's labor-based grading contracts that take into consideration students' engagement but still depend upon a normative concept of labor.

Focusing on engagement rather than labor also addresses my contention that labor-based grading contracts perpetuate a normative conception of time, as well as the unnecessary and unfounded connection between time and willingness. Students may have the will to labor, but they may not have the time to do so. This is often a socioeconomic issue that limits how inclusive labor-based grading contracts actually are. It is also a (dis)ability issue. If students are allowed to choose the form of engagement that is suitable and possible for them at a particular moment in time, that can help bridge willingness and ability. As Tara Wood (2017, 267) points out, "One way (not *the* way) to increase accessibility in composition classrooms is to rethink our conceptions of time." She explains further, "Because accommodation models are so heavily tied to time and considering that the most common accommodations (extended exam time) are often futile in writing classrooms—we need a paradigmatic shift in the ways we construct time for our students." Although not writing about grading contracts, what Wood says about time, from a disability studies perspective, is especially relevant. Labor-based grading contracts are beholden to what Wood calls "normative, compulsory time frames" that "may contribute to or unproductively exacerbate anxiety" (270). Wood says we need, instead, to approach the construction of time in writing classrooms in such a way that "doesn't rely on compulsory able-bodiedness" (269–270).

In disability studies this concept is called crip time, which Margaret Price (2011, 63) describes as a more flexible approach to time than is usually present in the education system in which "students are expected to arrive on time, absorb information at a particular speed, and perform spontaneously in restricted time frames." Crip time recognizes that people move, engage, and process information at different rates and speeds. In her study of thirty-five students with both documented and undocumented disabilities, Wood (2017, 270) found that "'students' anxiety might be alleviated through cripping time, increasing flexibility, avoiding rigidity, and lowering the stakes of writing (particularly in the beginning stages of a course)." This more inclusive and flexible approach to assessment, captured by an engagement-based grading contract, would address the ableist aspects of labor-based grading contracts.

As Kryger and Zimmerman (2020) point out, less dependence on a normative conception of time and its relationship to labor would benefit neurodivergent students, in particular, who

> frequently need to perform vastly different quantities and types of labor to accomplish the same academic performance. For example, anxiety or depression can cause students to struggle to maintain sustained effort on a task; ADHD can require a student to read a passage multiple times to gain the same benefit as a neurotypical student due to difficulties in managing attention; autistic students may need assistance to produce expected levels of linguistic expression on assignments; and dyslexic students may need to access materials through differentiated technologies that require additional time investments. In each of these cases, neurodivergent students often invest more embodied/physical and emotional/affective labor toward completing the cognitive labor than a neurotypical peer but are provided the same reward for these arguably more extensive efforts.

Moreover, because "labor-tracking activity may produce a deficit model for neurodivergent students who are already deeply aware of how their laboring differs from the normative population" (n.p.), Kryger and Zimmerman "encourage instructors to consider how their conceptions of labor, and specifically time, offer (de)limiting experiences for our neurodivergent student populations" (n.p.).

Reconceiving of time in the ways Wood describes and for the reasons Kryger and Zimmerman outline just above seems especially productive when it comes to rethinking grading contracts because it necessarily "requires that teachers relax their hold on the boundaries of time" and "requires some relinquishment of authority" (Wood 2017, 280, 281). Relinquishing teacherly authority in order to share it with students is often an impetus for adopting grading contracts anyway. Exploring with students how to crip time in order to create an assessment ecology that doesn't adhere to normative time would increase inclusivity. Moreover, cripping time would challenge the rigid and normative conceptions of time that characterize not only labor-based contract grading practices but the labor logs that are often part of this ecology, as well as the assignments that spell out the expected time on task for each assignment. Ultimately, replacing labor with engagement and introducing crip time into the classroom would allow for the decoupling of willingness and ability because a student's chosen form of engagement is not bound to normative conceptions of time. For example, a student might choose to engage in the course by posting on the discussion board instead of completing a longer response paper one week because they needed to take on extra hours at their job. Within this framework, that student's willingness to participate in the class is not impeded by their need to work extra hours at their job or by normative conceptions of time that demand a predetermined amount of time on task.

Labor-based grading contracts don't totally discount the outside forces that might interfere with students' labor. Inoue (2019, 222), for example, notes that "the ecology does not control the outside forces that limit students' time. At least in a labor-based grading contract ecology," Inoue continues, "we can pay better attention and account for the labor and time we are asking of students, and not hide behind standards and claims that we 'don't grade based on effort.'" What I am suggesting, though, goes at least one step further by introducing nonnormative concepts of time into the classroom upon which students' levels of engagement depend. In other words, in the kind of engagement-based grading contract I am describing, students are not bound by the specific tasks that are attached to a normative estimate of time on task.

## DRAWING ON SCHOLARSHIP IN LINGUISTIC
## JUSTICE TO CREATE ASSESSMENTS

While I have relied on scholarship and research from disability studies to anchor my discussion thus far, Jerry Won Lee's work on linguistic justice is also helpful. Lee (2016, 186) argues for an almost entirely individualized approach to evaluation, what he describes as "translanguaging assessment," which involves "continuously individualizing the criteria by which student writing is evaluated, working beyond a homogeneous set of standards, even for one particular classroom." This form of assessment invites students to reflect on and choose how they would like their writing to be assessed. This separates Lee's approach from Inoue's because Lee is willing to provide access to the White, dominant standard discourse if that is what an individual student wants. Lee (2016) explains: "We need to find ways to guide our students to make decisions that make the most sense for them and, through our assessment practices, evaluate their work on the basis of what the student believes is in the best interest for short-term and long-term goals. . . . There will be students who wish to focus on developing their proficiency in a standardized variety of English. But it is these same students who will often be penalized for not having this set of skills upon arriving to the classroom" (188). Although grounded in a translingual orientation toward writing, Lee's approach has applications that extend far beyond this context. While not explicitly discussing grading contracts, we can adapt Lee's approach, which offers an alternative to community/ classroom-based grading contracts. When we adapt Lee's argument to contract grading, the contract ceases to be between the teacher and the class as a whole and is, instead, between the teacher and each individual student. If students are conscientiously prepared to engage in individual contract negotiations and to stand up for what they value, this approach would mitigate many of the problems that labor-based grading contracts pose for students who are not the normative, able-bodied, neurotypical student at their center.

Admittedly, such an individualized approach to assessment has its drawbacks. First, this approach could mean starting from scratch with individual students, which may increase the labor on the part of the teacher, thereby undermining one of the benefits of labor-based contract grading. Starting from scratch and working with individual students, though, has its own benefits that have been lauded by followers of Malcolm S. Knowles's concept of self-directed learning in the 1970s and the "learning contracts" he developed with students. Working from scratch—whether with a full class or individual students—could mitigate some of the resistance students report feeling toward grading contracts, which supposedly give them a voice in how they are assessed but are usually created by the instructor and only allowed to be negotiated by students. This "from scratch" approach also increases the potential for inclusivity because the contracts are co-created by students who, if adequately prepared to engage in negotiations with an instructor, could ensure that the contract meets their needs. While students who negotiate their contracts on an individual basis would lose out on the benefits of participating in a community-based negotiation, students would gain the opportunity to co-create an assessment practice that values what they value, which seems like a fair tradeoff to me. As such, I would argue that the benefits of grading contracts based on Lee's notion of translingual assessment outweigh these drawbacks precisely because this form of assessment "attend[s] to student aspirations on an individual level rather than merely reacting to disciplinary trends (for instance, encouraging students to produce translingual writing)" (185).

Moreover, explains Lee (2016, 185), "translanguaging assessment is not simply a call to adapt assessment criteria to value 'translingual' writing more; it is about de-universalizing assessment criteria so we remember that different kinds of writing have different values for different students." The need to de-universalize assessment criteria is at the core of what labor-based grading contracts strive to do but ultimately cannot because of the normative conceptions of labor and time that inform them.

The two potential ways forward I have outlined here, as well as those I have alluded to throughout this essay, offer some possibilities for expanding current iterations of labor-based grading contracts with the goal of greater inclusivity. As Mya Poe, Asao Inoue, and Nobert Elliot (2018, 5) point out in their collection titled *Writing Assessment, Social Justice, and the Advancement of Opportunity*, "As a form of research, writing assessment best serves students when justice is taken as the ultimate aim of assessment; once adopted, that aim advances assessment as a principled way to create individual opportunity through identification of opportunity structures." As a field, writing studies is fortunate to encompass such a rich and diverse set of theories and practices that offer multiple lenses through which to imagine how we can create these opportunities for all students. A disability studies orientation toward assessment exposes the biases that remain in labor-based contract grading, thereby laying the foundation for reshaping and reimagining more inclusive approaches to this form of assessment. Similarly, using a translingual lens through which to view assessment opens up possibilities for incorporating more student agency into assessments so that students are not penalized for lacking proficiency in a standardized form of English, but are simultaneously given access to that standardized form if they so desire. Finally, the interdisciplinary nature of writing studies allows us to draw on

Kimberlé Crenshaw's concept of intersectionality to expose the hidden inequities in labor-based grading contracts that potentially harm students with intersecting identities.

In closing, I'll return to where I began: the pandemic. With the COVID-19 pandemic further underscoring inequities within the educational system, it is imperative to think about ways to move toward more socially just forms of education that address the biases—racial and otherwise—inherent in the assessment practices upon which the system depends. Conceiving of inclusive education "not as an *outcome* that must be achieved" but "as a *process* that is always ongoing, continual, and by extension, unfinished" (Danforth and Naraian 2015, 72; emphasis in original), we must continue these conversations within writing studies, which while richly diverse in its theoretical approaches proudly continues to put students at its center.

# References

American College Health Association. 2019. "ACHA-National College Health Assessment III Fall 2019 Reference Group Summary." https://www.acha.org/documents/ncha/NCHAII_Spring_2018 _Undergraduate_Reference_Group_Executive_Summary.pdf.

Bailey, Moya, and Izetta Autumn Mobley. 2019. "A Black Feminist Disability Framework." *Gender and Society* 33 (1): 19–40.

Banks, Joy. 2014. "Barriers and Supports to Postsecondary Transition: Case Studies of African American Students with Disabilities." *Remedial and Special Education* 35: 28–39. https://doi.org/10 .1177/0741932513512209.

Banks, Joy, and Michael S. Hughes. 2013. "Double Consciousness: Postsecondary Experiences of African American Males with Disabilities." *The Journal of Negro Education* 82 (4): 368–381. https://doi .org/10.7709/jnegroeducation.82.4.0368.

Bessaha, Melissa, Rebecca Reed, Amanda J. Donlon, Wendi Mathews, Alissa C. Bell, and Danielle Merolla. 2020. "Creating a More Inclusive Environment for Students with Disabilities: Findings from Participatory Action Research." *Disability Studies Quarterly* 40 (3). https://dsq-sds.org/article/view/7094/5708.

Blackstock, Alan, and Virginia Norris Exton. 2014. "'Space to Grow': Grading Contracts for Basic Writers." *Teaching English in the Two-Year College* 41(3): 278–293.

Browning, Ella R. 2014. "Disability Studies in the Composition Classroom." *Composition Studies* 42 (2): 96–117.

Breneman, Daisy L., Susan Ghiaciuc, Valerie L. Schoolcraft, and Keri A. Vendeberg. 2017. "I Am Different / So Are You: Creating Safe Spaces for Disability Disclosure (A Conversation)." In *Negotiating Disability: Disclosure and Higher Education*, edited by Stephanie L. Kerschbaum, Laura T. Eisenman, and James M. Jones, 345–362. Ann Arbor: University of Michigan Press.

Bridgland, Victoria M. E., Ella K. Moeck, Deanne M. Green, Taylor L. Swain, Diane M. Nayda, Lucy A. Matson, Nadine P. Hutchison, Melanie K. T. Takarangi. 2021. "Why the COVID-19 Pandemic is a Traumatic Stressor." *PLoS ONE* 16 (1): 1–15. https://doi.org/10.1371/journal.pone.0240146.

Brueggemann, Brenda Jo. 2001. "An Enabling Pedagogy: Meditations on Writing and Disability." *JAC* 21 (4): 791–820.

Brueggemann, Brenda Jo, Linda Feldmeier White, Patricia A. Dunn, Barbara A. Heifferon and Johnson Cheu. 2001. "Becoming Visible: Lessons in Disability." *CCC* 52 (3): 368–398.

Cedillo, Christina V. 2020. "Disabled and Undocumented: In/Visibility at the Borders of Presence, Disclosure, and Nation." *Rhetoric Society Quarterly* 50 (3): 203–211.

Center for Collegiate Mental Health. 2020. "2019 Annual Report." University Park, PA: Penn State University. https://ccmh.memberclicks.net/assets/docs/2019-CCMH-Annual-Report_3.17.20.pdf.

Cowan, Michelle. 2020. "A Legacy of Grading Contracts for Composition." *Journal of Writing Assessment* 13 (2). http://journalofwritingassessment.org/article.php?article=150.

Danforth, Scot, and Srikala Naraian. 2015. "This New Field of Inclusive Education: Beginning a Dialogue on Conceptual Foundations." *Intellectual and Developmental Disabilities* 53 (1): 70–85.

Danielewicz, Jane, and Peter Elbow. 2009. "A Unilateral Grading Contract to Improve Teaching and Learning." *College Composition and Communication* 61 (2): 244–267.

Dartmouth College. 2020. "COVID-19 Increased Anxiety, Depression for Already Stressed College Students." Press release. https://www.dartmouth.edu/press-releases/covid-19-stressed-college-students.html.

Dolmage, Jay. 2006. "Mapping Composition." In *Disability and the Teaching of Writing: A Critical Sourcebook*, edited by Cindy Lewiecki-Wilson and Brenda Brueggemann, 14–27. Boston: Bedford St. Martin's.

Dolmage, Jay Timothy. 2014. *Disability Rhetoric*. Syracuse: Syracuse University Press.

Dolmage, Jay T. 2017. *Academic Ableism: Disability and Higher Education*. Ann Arbor: University of Michigan Press.

Eisenberg, Daniel, Sarah Ketchen Lipson, and Justin Heinze. 2020. "The Healthy Minds Study: Fall 2020 Data Report." https://ccmh .memberclicks.net/assets/docs/2019-CCMH-Annual-Report_3 .17.20.pdf.

Elbow, Peter. 2006. "Do We Need a Single Standard of Value for Institutional Assessment? An Essay Response to Asao Inoue's 'Community-Based Assessment Pedagogy?'" *Assessing Writing* 11: 81–99.

Fruehwirth, Jane Cooley, Siddhartha Biswas, and Krista M. Perreira. 2021. "The Covid-19 Pandemic and Mental Health of First-Year College Students: Examining the Effect of Covid-19 Stressors Using Longitudinal Data." *PLoS ONE* 16 (3): 1–15. https://doi .org/10.1371/journal.pone.0247999.

Garland-Thomson, Rosemarie. 1996. *Extraordinary Bodies: Figuring Physical Disability in American Culture and Life*. New York: Columbia University Press.

Gomes, Mathew, Bree Bellati, Mia Hope, and Alissa LaFerriere. 2020. "Enabling Meaningful Labor: Narratives of Participation in a Grading Contract." *Journal of Writing Assessment* 13 (2). http:// journalofwritingassessment.org/article.php?article=152.

Hampton, Nan Zhang, and Seneca E. Sharp. 2013. "Shame-Focused Attitudes toward Mental Health Problems: The Role of Gender and Culture." *Rehabilitation Counseling Bulletin* 57 (3): 170–181.

Harbour, Wendy S., Rosalie Boone, Elaine Bourne Heath, and Sislena G. Ledbetter. 2017. "'Overcoming' in Disability Studies and African American Culture: Implications for Higher Education." In *Negotiating Disability: Disclosure and Higher Education*, edited by Stephanie L. Kerschbaum, Laura T. Eisenman, and James M. Jones, 149–170. Ann Arbor: University of Michigan Press.

Hassel, Holly. 2013. "Research Gaps in Teaching English in the Two-Year College." *Teaching English in the Two-Year College* 40 (4): 343–363.

Hitt, Allison Harper. 2021. *Rhetorics of Overcoming: Rewriting Narratives of Disability and Accessibility in Writing Studies*. Champaign, IL: NCTE.

Inman, Joyce O., and Rebecca A. Powell. 2018. "In the Absence of Grades: Dissonance and Desire in Course-Contract Classrooms." *College Composition and Communication* 70 (1): 30–56.

Inoue, Asao B. 2012. "Grading Contracts: Assessing their Effectiveness on Different Racial Formations." In *Race and Writing Assessment*, edited by Asao B. Inoue and Mya Poe, 78–93. New York: Peter Lang.

Inoue, Asao B. 2019. *Labor Based Grading Contracts: Building Equity and Inclusion in the Compassionate Writing Classroom*. Fort Collins, CO: WAC Clearinghouse/University Press of Colorado. https://wac.colostate.edu/docs/books/labor/contracts.pdf.

Kerschbaum, Stephanie L. 2014. "On Rhetorical Agency and Disclosing Disability in Academic Writing." *Rhetoric Review* 33 (1): 55–71. DOI: 10.1080/07350198.2014.856730.

Kerschbaum, Stephanie L. 2015. "Anecdotal Relations: On Orienting to Disability in the Composition Classroom." *Composition Forum* 32. https://compositionforum.com/issue/32/anecdotal-relations.php.

Kerschbaum, Stephanie L., Amber M. O'Shea, Margaret Price, and Mark S. Salzer. 2017. "Accommodations and Disclosure for Faculty members with Mental Disability." In *Negotiating Disability: Disclosure and Higher Education*, edited by Stephanie L. Kerschbaum, Laura T. Eisenman, and James M. Jones, 311–326. Ann Arbor: University of Michigan Press.

King, Carolyne M. 2019. "The Reader in the Textbook: Embodied Materiality and Reading in the Writing Classroom." *Composition Studies* 47 (1): 95–115.

Konrad, Annika. 2021. "Access Fatigue: The Rhetorical Work of Disability in Everyday Life." *College English* 83 (3): 180–199.

Krebs, Emily. 2019. "Baccalaureates or Burdens? Complicating 'Reasonable Accommodations' for American College Students with Disabilities." *Disability Studies Quarterly* 39 (3). https://dsq-sds.org/article/view/6557/5413.

Kryger, Kathleen, and Griffin X. Zimmerman. 2020. "A Legacy of Grading Contracts for Composition." *Journal of Writing Assessment* 13 (2). http://journalofwritingassessment.org/article.php?article=150.

Lee, Jerry Won. 2016. "Beyond Translingual Writing." *College English* 79 (2): 174–195.

Lewiecki-Wilson, Cynthia, and Brenda Jo Brueggeman. 2008. *Disability and the Teaching of Writing: A Critical Sourcebook*. Boston, MA: Bedford/St. Martin's.

Litterio, Lisa M. 2016. "Contract Grading in a Technical Writing Class-room: A Case Study." *The Journal of Writing Assessment* 9 (2). http://journalofwritingassessment.org/article.php?article=101.

Low, Jacqueline. 1996. "Negotiating Identities, Negotiating Environ-ment: An Interpretation of Experiences of Students with Disabili-ties." *Disability & Society* 11 (2): 235–248.

Madaus, Joseph W., Nicholas W. Gelbar, Lyman L. Dukes III, Michael N. Faggella-Luby, Eileen Glavey, and Annette Romualdo. 2021. "Stu-dents with Disabilities in the Community College Professional Literature: A Systematic Review." *Community College Journal of Research and Practice*, 45 (1): 31–40.

Maier, Sophia, V. Jo Hsu, Christina V Cedillo, and M. Remi Yergeau. 2020. "GET THE FRAC IN! Or, The Fractal Many-festo: A (Trans)(Crip)t." *Peitho* 22 (4). https://cfshrc.org/article/get-the-frac-in-or-the-fractal-many-festo-a-transcript/.

McKee, Aja, and Audri Sandoval Gomez. 2020. "The Voices of Typers: Examining the Educational Experiences of Individuals Who Use Facilitated Communication." *Disability Studies Quarterly* 40 (4).

Medina, Cruz, and Kenneth Walker. 2018. "Validating the Consequences of a Social Justice Pedagogy." In *Key Theoretical Frameworks: Teaching Technical Communication in the Twenty-First Century*, edited by Angela M. Haas and Michelle F. Eble, 46–67. Louisville: University Press of Colorado.

Miller, Ryan A., Richmond D. Wynn, and Kristine W. Webb. 2017. "Complicating 'Coming Out': Disclosing Disability, Gender, and Sexuality in Higher Education." In *Negotiating Disability: Disclo-sure and Higher Education*, edited by Stephanie L. Kerschbaum, Laura T. Eisenman, and James M. Jones, 115–134. Ann Arbor: University of Michigan Press.

Mingus, Mia. 2011. "Access Intimacy: The Missing Link." *Leaving Evi-dence* (blog). May 5, 2011. https://leavingevidence.wordpress.com/2011/05/05/access-intimacy-the-missing-link/.

Morgan, Paul L., George Farkas, Marianne Hillemeier, and Steve Maczuga. 2017. "Replicated Evidence of Racial and Ethnic Disparities in Disability Identification in U.S. Schools." *Edu-cational Researcher* 46 (6): 305–322. https://doi.org/10.3102%2F0013189X17726282.

Newman, Lynn, Mary Wagner, Anne-Marie Knokey, Camille Marder, Katherine Nagle, Deborah Shaver, and Xin Wei. 2011. "The

Post-High School Outcomes of Young Adults with Disabilities up to 8 Years After High School. A Report from the National Longitudinal Transition Study-2 (NLTS2)." National Center for Special Education Research. Menlo Park, CA: SRI International. https://files.eric.ed.gov/fulltext/ED524044.pdf.

Nuru-Jeter, Amani M., Roland H. Thorpe Jr., and Esme Fuller-Thomson. 2011. "Black-White Differences in Self-Reported Disability Outcomes in the U.S.: Early Childhood to Older Adulthood." *Published Health Reports* 126 (6): 834–843. https://doi.org/10.1177%2F003335491112600609.

Pearson, Holly, and Lisa Boskovich. 2019. "Problematizing Disability Disclosure in Higher Education: Shifting Towards a Liberating Humanizing Intersectional Framework." *Disability Studies Quarterly 39 (1)*. https://dsq-sds.org/article/view/6001.

Pellegrino, Amanda M., Beverly M. Sermons, and George W. Shaver. 2011. "Disproportionality Among Postsecondary Students Seeking Evaluation to Document Disabilities." *Disability Studies Quarterly* 31 (2). https://dsq-sds.org/article/view/1588/1556.

Petersen, Amy J. 2009. " 'Ain't Nobody Gonna Get Me Down': An Examination of the Educational Experiences of Four African American Women Labeled with Disabilities." *Equity and Excellence in Education* 42 (2): 428–442. https://doi.org/10.1080/10665680903245284.

Poe, Mya, Asao B. Inoue, and Nobert Elliot. 2018. *Writing Assessment, Social Justice and the Advancement of Opportunity*. Fort Collins: The WAC Clearinghouse/University Press of Colorado. https://doi.org/10.37514/PER-B.2018.0155.

Potts, Glenda. 2010. "A Simple Alternative to Grading." *Inquiry* 15 (1): 29–42.

Price, Margaret. 2011. *Mad at School: Rhetorics of Mental Disability and Academic Life*. Ann Arbor: University of Michigan Press.

Prowse, S. 2009. "Institutional Construction of Disabled Students." *Journal of Higher Education Policy and Management* 31 (1): 89–96.

Rocco, Tonette S., and Joshua C. Collins. 2017. "An Initial Model for Accommodation Communication between Students with Disabilities and Faculty." In *Negotiating Disability: Disclosure and Higher Education*, edited by Stephanie L. Kerschbaum, Laura T. Eisenman, and James M. Jones, 327–344. Ann Arbor: University of Michigan Press.

Rule, Hannah J. 2017. "Sensing the Sentence: An Embodied Simulation Approach to Rhetorical Grammar." *Composition Studies* 45 (1): 19–38.

Shor, Ira. 1996. *When Students Have Power: Negotiating Authority in a Critical Pedagogy*. Chicago, IL. University of Chicago Press.

Shor, Ira, Eugene Matusov, Ana Marjanovic-Shane, and James Cresswell. 2017. "Dialogic & Critical Pedagogies: An Interview with Ira Shor." *Dialogic Pedagogy: An International Online Journal* 5. http://dpj.pitt.edu. DOI: 10.5195/dpj.2017.208.

Son, Changwon, Sudeep Hegde, Alec Smith, Xiaomei Wang, and Farzan Sasangohar. 2020. "Effects of COVID-19 on College Students' Mental Health in the United States: Interview Survey Study." *Journal of Medical Internet Research* 22 (9). https://www.ncbi.nlm.nih.gov/pmc/articles/PMC7473764/#ref13. doi: 10.2196/21279.

Steinmetz, Katy. 2020. "She Coined the Term 'Intersectionality' Over 30 Years Ago. Here's What It Means to Her Today." *Time*, February 20, 2020. https://time.com/5786710/kimberle-crenshaw-intersectionality/.

Tayles. Melissa. 2020. "Trauma-Informed Writing Pedagogy: Ways to Support Student Writers Affected by Trauma and Traumatic Stress." *Teaching English in the Two-Year College* 48 (3): 295–313.

Thelin, William H., and Cathy Spidell. 2006. "Not Ready to Let Go: A Study of Resistance to Grading Contracts." *Composition Studies* 34 (1): 35–68.

Timmerman, Lorna C., and Thalia M. Mulvihill. 2015. "Accommodations in the College Setting: The Perspectives of Students Living with Disabilities." *The Qualitative Report* 20 (10): 1609–1625.

Tucker, Phebe, and Christopher Czapla S. 2021. "Post-COVID Stress Disorder: Another Emerging Consequence of the Global Pandemic." *Psychiatric Times* 38 (1). https://www.psychiatrictimes.com/view/post-covid-stress-disorder-emerging-consequence-global-pandemic.

US Department of Education. 2019. National Center for Educational Statistics. https://nces.ed.gov/fastfacts/display.asp?id=60.

Villanueva, Nayelee Uzan. 2014. "*Impact of a Grade Contract Model in a Basic Writing Composition Course: A Qualitative Multiple Case Study*." PhD diss., University of Nevada, Las Vegas. https://digitalscholarship.unlv.edu/thesesdissertations/2308/.

Wood, Shane. 2020. "Book Review: Labor-Based Grading Contracts:
    Building Equity and Inclusion in the Writing Classroom by
    Asao B. Inoue." *The Journal of Writing Assessment* 13 (1). http://
    journalofwritingassessment.org/article.php?article=142.
Wood, Tara. 2017. "Cripping Time in the Composition Classroom."
    *College Composition and Communication* 69 (2): 260–286.
Yergeau, M. Remi. 2018. *Authoring Autism: On Rhetoric and Neurological
    Queerness*. Durham, NC: Duke University Press.

# About the Author

**Ellen C. Carillo** is professor of English at the University of Connecticut and the writing coordinator at its Waterbury Campus. She is the author of *Securing a Place for Reading in Composition: The Importance of Teaching for Transfer* (Utah State UP, 2015); *A Writer's Guide to Mindful Reading* (WAC Clearinghouse/University Press of Colorado, 2017); *Teaching Readers in Post-Truth America* (Utah State UP, 2018); the *MLA Guide to Digital Literacy* (Modern Language Association, 2019); as well as editor of *Reading Critically, Writing Well*, 12th edition (Bedford/St. Martin's, 2019) and *Reading and Writing Instruction in the Twenty-First Century: Recovering and Transforming the Pedagogy of Robert Scholes* (Utah State UP, 2021). She is co-editor of *Teaching Critical Reading and Writing in the Era of Fake News* (Peter Lang, 2020) and *The St. Martin's Guide to Writing*, 13th edition (Bedford/St. Martin's, 2021). Her scholarship has also been published in many journals and edited collections. Ellen is co-founder of the Role of Reading in Composition Studies Special Interest Group of the Conference on College Composition and Communication (CCCC) and regularly presents her research at regional and national conferences. She has been awarded grants from the Northeast Modern Language Association (NeMLA), CCCC, and the Council of Writing Program Administrators (CWPA).